STORYWORLDS

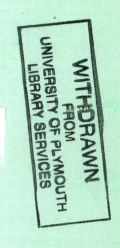
Ideas for teaching Primary Geography using 10 popular children's stories

ISBN 1 873928 58 0

Humanities Education Centre,
Tower Hamlets Professional Development Centre,
English St., London E3 4TA
Tel. 0181 981 0183 Fax 0181 981 9956

AIM OF THE BOOK

This book aims to provide activities to support the teaching of Key Stages 1 and 2 Geography for the National Curriculum Revised Orders (1995). It is based upon ten popular children's storybooks.

The activities support and promote Development Education values and approaches to learning and teaching.

According to HM Inspectorate's discussion series *Curriculum Matters*

"... geographical studies should help pupils to :

- develop a strong interest in their own surroundings and in the world as the home of mankind (sic)

- understand some of the relationships between people and environments

- understand what it means to live in one place rather than another

- appreciate the significance of people's beliefs, attitudes and values to those relationships and issues which have a geographical dimension

- construct a framework of knowledge and understanding about their home area, about their own country and about other parts of the world, which will enable them to place information within appropriate geographical contexts."

HOW TO USE THE BOOK

Each story has been given two pages of coverage which includes an abstract, activities and a vocabulary table showing geographical vocabulary at Key Stages 1 and 2 that can be learned through the use of the story.

The story matrix on page 5 shows which parts of the National Curriculum Revised Orders for Geography are supported by each particular story.

CONTENTS

INTRODUCTION

by Yolanda Wisewitch

The stories chosen for this book cover the range of requirements outlined in the National Curriculum Key Stage 2 Programme of Study. Many of the stories and activities are also suitable at Key Stage 1.

The National Curriculum requirement for the study of places requires that children contrast their own locality with two others : - one in the UK and and another in an economically developing country.

'Masai and I' and *'A Balloon for Grandad'* present such contrasts as an integral part of the story. *'The People Who Hugged the Trees'* provides an excellent opportunity for non-British locality comparison, with *'Katie Morag Delivers the Mail'* and *'Bear's Adventure'* both offering a British non-urban locality.

The National Curriculum at Key Stage 2 requires

that four themes should be investigated and that these should be studied within the context of actual places. *'Where the River Begins'* would make a motivating start to the topic of **rivers**, whilst a study on **weather** could be initiated with *'Bringing the Rain to Kapiti Plain'*.

Environmental change is clearly illustrated using the story *'Shaker Lane'* and although many of the stories fit the **settlement theme**, the stories *'Somewhere in Africa'* and *'The Day of Ahmed's Secret'* go further by challenging preconceptions of what it is like to live in Africa.

The number of activities suggested for each story offers the teacher the choice of either fully exploring one story, or mixing and matching a number of stories in order to teach geographical skills and topic requirements.

GEOGRAPHY THROUGH STORY

A story's power lies in its ability to enthuse and motivate children, making geography easier and more accessible to all pupils. Choosing a story, sharing it, then following it up with challenging, meaningful activities provides an excellent means for delivering the geography curriculum.

Some reasons for using storybooks to teach geography in the primary school have been put forward in the HM Inspectorate's document Geography from 5-16

> *Once their interest has been aroused, pupils can be encouraged and helped to find out more about the lives of people living in different places. Such studies are more likely to be successful when pupils have access to appropriate artefacts, photographs and stories which engage their imaginations.*

and the following

> *...good stories, with distinct settings, can*

stimulate an interest in environments which are very different from their [young pupils] own. Such stories, especially when accompanied by suitable drawings or photographs can provide children with powerful images of particular places and some sense of what it is like to live there. They can be a means of introducing children to cultures which are different from their own and of encouraging an understanding and respect for other people's beliefs, aspirations and styles of living.

PREPARE FOR SUCCESS

Stories have the power to capture and motivate our thinking

- They take us places we could never hope to visit, providing us with insights to experiences we could never otherwise have.

- They can mirror our everyday life, encouraging us to take a fresh look at what we take for granted.

- They are a valuable part of our culture, and in the classroom situation, are enjoyed by children and teachers alike.

It is perhaps children's obvious enjoyment of a story that makes it a powerful tool for the teacher in motivating pupil's interest and enthusiasm in geography. It encourages and excites children's natural curiosity about the world, both their own world, and that of others.

Children bring a wide range of experiences and geographical knowledge with them when they come to school. Story can provide opportunities for children to meet again with what is familiar and known to them. It both confirms their understanding and validates their experiences as important, worthy of discussion.

It also offers the children an opportunity to learn about the lives of others and about places that they can not have direct experience of, thus extending their understandings beyond their community to the world.

SPECIAL NEEDS

Whether the particular story is familiar or not, the experience of story reading is a known "safe" activity that children will have enjoyed many times. The children know what to expect, it is part of everyday class and home life.

Thus it is particularly useful for children with special needs as a means of introducing what is new, in a format which is known and safe.

Storytelling is something all teachers are experienced in doing, and is something that most teachers do well. It's *"the known"* for us as well. And so both the teacher and the children are prepared for success when using story for work in geography.

Further, there is a particular advantage with picture books in their ability to convey messages through visual images, heightening, or even completely providing the meaning of the story for those to whom the language is inaccessible.

LANGUAGE ACQUISITION

It is vital for the learner in exploring geographical skills and concepts to have the vocabulary to do so.

Stories provide children with these key words and language, thus enabling them to most effectively pose questions and discuss their topic using the appropriate terminology. The children take on the vocabulary as they enjoy the story; its meaning enhanced by pictures, context and discussion.

The National Curriculum states *"that at Key Stage 2 pupils should be taught to use appropriate geographical vocabulary to describe and interpret their surroundings".*

PLANNING FOR GEOGRAPHY THROUGH STORY

Learning activities should be planned for what the children need to know, not for what the book can cover. It is important to ensure that the story fits the teaching objectives, not vice versa, so that the learning is meaningful and fits in with what is required by the National Curriculum.

Care should be taken not to overwork the story to the point where the children (and teacher) lose sight of the main objectives.

Some objectives given by the aforementioned Curriculum Matters apply particularly to geography through story and we mention them below.

OBJECTIVES FOR THE GEOGRAPHY CURRICULUM

The curriculum should provide pupils with learning experiences of a geographical nature that will enable them to:

EARLY PRIMARY YEARS

- *...extend their awareness of, and develop their interest in, their surroundings;*

- *begin to develop an interest in people and places beyond their immediate experience;*

- *develop an awareness of cultural and ethnic diversity within our society, while recognising the similarity of activities, interests and aspirations of different people.*

LATER PRIMARY YEARS

- *Study some aspects of life and conditions in a number of other small areas in Britain and abroad, which provide comparisons with their own locality. From such studies pupils should gain knowledge and understanding of some of the ways in which people have used, modified and cared for their surroundings, and of the influence of environmental conditions, cultures and technology on the activities and ways of life of the present inhabitants;*

- *develop an appreciation of the many life styles in Britain and abroad, which reflect a variety of cultures, and develop positive attitudes towards different communities and societies, countering racial and cultural stereotyping and prejudice.*

PREPARING CHILDREN FOR GLOBAL CITIZENSHIP
A definition of Development Education

Development Education is defined by UNICEF as education ...

"which promotes the development in young people of values of global solidarity, peace, tolerance, social justice and environmental awareness and equips them with the knowledge and skills that empower them to participate effectively in promoting those values. It does so by providing a framework of global concepts applicable to a wide variety of themes and topics and a learning process that proceeds from knowledge to action. It has evolved from being education about the problems of developing countries to a broader concept of education for global citizenship."

THE STORY MATRIX

NATIONAL CURRICULUM REQUIREMENTS	A Balloon for Grandad	Bear's Adventure	Bringing the Rain to Kapiti Plain	The Day of Ahmed's Secret	Katie Morage Delivers the Mail	Masai and I	The People Who Hugged the Trees	Shaker Lane	Somewhere in Africa	Where the River Begins
Undertake fieldwork	○	●			●		○	●		●
Making and using of maps	●	●	○	○	●	●	○	●	○	○
Use of secondary sources	○	●	○	●	●	○	●	●	○	○
Local area	●	○		○	○	○	●	●	●	●
UK contrast to local area	○	●	○		●				●	●
Non-UK contrast to local area	●		●	●		●	●	○	●	○
Rivers	○			○						●
Weather	○		●	○			●		●	●
Settlement	●	○	○	●	●	●	○	●	●	○
Environmental change	○		○	○			●	●	○	○

● strongly supports   ○ supports

A BALLOON FOR GRANDAD

THE STORY

Sam loses his balloon, the wind takes it far away. Sam's father consoles him with a tale about the balloon travelling to his Grandad Abdullah over mountains, seas, deserts and rivers. They imagine the balloon finally arriving having journeyed over many different countries and environments.

QUESTIONS AND DISCUSSION

Why does Sam live in a different country to his grandad?

Why do people move to other countries?

MAPPING

Grandad Abdullah lives overseas.

- Do a survey to find out how many pupils have friends or family who live abroad.

- Label the countries where they live on a wall map and find out more about them.
  (Some sensitivity should be used with this exercise - best to do in a class where lots of children have relatives abroad).

Look at the overhead view of Grandad Abdullah's island in the river.

- Make a representation in map form with symbols to identify main features.

Look at an aerial photograph of the local area.

- Draw a map of the local area with symbols.

- Compare with the map of grandad's island and find similarities and differences.

- Compare the local aerial photograph and children's maps with an ordnance survey map of the area. Identify features common to each other.

- Choose one of the maps to chart the possible route a balloon may take if let go in the school grounds.
  Find out about wind direction in planning its route.

- Investigate and map a possible route that the balloon might take from school to a place similar to where Grandad Abdullah lives.

- Make a list of other possible destinations and map a route over towns, mountains, seas, deserts and rivers to these places.

DESERT

- List all the countries with desert environments. Choose one country to do a locality study of a desert environment.

- For the chosen locality, investigate climate, rainfall, sunshine, exports, population, etc., using thematic maps and tables.
  Investigate the effect of people on their environment, considering resources such as food and water and activities such as employment, health, education, transport, lifestyle etc.

- Chart the findings of these investigations under 'positive', 'negative' or both aspects. Discuss the reasons.

EXPORTS

Grandad Abdullah grows dates.

- Bring dates and other unusual fruits for the children to taste.
  Label a world map showing where each fruit comes from.

- Visit the supermarket and find out what is grown here and what comes from abroad.

  Find out how the produce gets here.

- Chart the story of a fruit from growing on a tree through all the stages involved to being put on the dining table.

- What produce does the UK export?

- On a world map, label all the countries where the UK's produce is exported.
  Compare with the map showing imports.

  Are any countries importing and exporting to the UK? Why might this be?

MOUNTAINS

- Investigate mountains and how they are shown on relief maps.

- List countries with mountains which children can locate on a relief map.

- Discuss how mountains are formed and how they age.

- Make a class model of the stages of a mountain's development.

Lisa

NATIONAL CURRICULUM VOCABULARY TABLE

KEY STAGE 1

PHYSICAL GEOGRAPHY	WEATHER & CLIMATE	SETTLEMENTS	TRANSPORT	ECONOMIC ACTIVITIES	LOCATIONAL WORDS
Cliff	Wind	Town	Journey	Shops	Map
Mountain	Snow	House		Supermarket	Country
Sea		Village			Position
River					Up/Down
Island					Aerial
Desert					photograph
Sand					

KEY STAGE 2

PHYSICAL GEOGRAPHY	WEATHER & CLIMATE	SETTLEMENTS	TRANSPORT	ECONOMIC ACTIVITIES	LOCATIONAL WORDS
Relief	Climate	Town	Routes	Import	Investigate
Landscape		House		Export	Symbols
Vegetation		Village		Market	
Features				Produce	
Environment				Employment	

BEAR'S ADVENTURE

THE STORY

A teddy bear is left on the beach by children. The bear floats away, sinks to the ocean bed, is caught in a fishing net and ends up on a fishing boat and then is dropped by a seagull back onto the beach.

QUESTIONS AND DISCUSSION

- What happens to things left on beaches or thrown away at sea?

- What is under the sea?

AERIAL PHOTOGRAPHS

- Look at an aerial photograph of your local area. List all the things you can see.

- Do the same for an aerial photograph of a small coastal town.

- Compare the two lists by circling all the features that are the same.

MAPPING

- Find out where the flags on the sand castle are from and locate on a map.

- Find flags of countries with which the children have connections and locate on a map.

WEATHER

- Discuss how the weather effects the fisherman's work, tourists etc.

- Discuss how the weather affects the school day i.e. playtime, outings, PE?

- Record the weather in the local area using measuring instruments such as thermometers and rain gauges .

BEACHES AND COASTS

- Visit a beach to collect shells.

- Discuss how sand is formed, the rocks on the coast and how the rivers flow to the sea.

- Look at the motion of waves and the rising and falling tide.

- Map the journey from school to the beach.

- Make a model of a coastline in a sand tray with sand dunes, houses, pier etc.

- Investigate what happens when water is washed against the sand.

- Make a map of the model coastline with a key.

- Use an atlas to find out how beaches and the sea are portrayed in maps.

- Investigate how their position is linked to the oceans and other islands.

- Using a globe or atlas and find countries that do not have a coastline e.g. Bolivia or Switzerland.

LIGHTHOUSES

- Make a model lighthouse with a torch. Darken the room and use the model to warn children where class furniture and other obstacles are as they try to cross the room.

- Make a display of flotsam and jetsam.

- Visit a local river/pond to collect or draw what is brought up.
  Compare with the beach flotsam and jetsam in the story.

JOBS

- Have the children been fishing? Discuss the similarities and differences between individual and company fishing.

- Have a whole class discussion or debate. Consider the issues surrounding fishing and the fish industry. Ask questions like :

  'Who eats the fish?'

  'What happens to it after it is caught?'

  'What are fish stocks?'

  'Do fish have rights?'

- The fisherman in this story live on the boat. What other jobs are there where workers live-in and why do they?

- Interview a live-in worker.

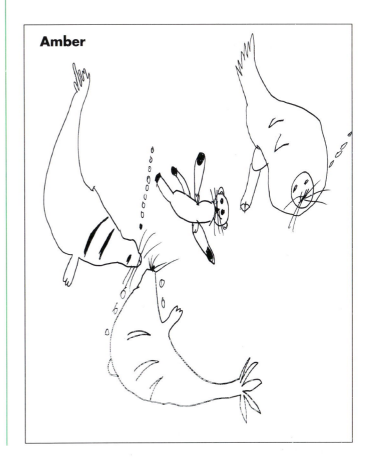

Amber

NATIONAL CURRICULUM VOCABULARY TABLE

KEY STAGE 1

PHYSICAL GEOGRAPHY	WEATHER & CLIMATE	SETTLEMENTS	TRANSPORT	ECONOMIC ACTIVITIES	LOCATIONAL WORDS
Sea	Rainbow	Castle	Boat	Fishing	Aerial
Waves	Cloud	Lighthouse	Road	Farm	photograph
Cliff	Summer	House	Journey		Map
Coast	Weather	Building			Country
Land		Town			
Sand dune		Village			
Beach					

KEY STAGE 2

PHYSICAL GEOGRAPHY	WEATHER & CLIMATE	SETTLEMENTS	TRANSPORT	ECONOMIC ACTIVITIES	LOCATIONAL WORDS
Tides	Temperature	Port		Natural	
Features	Rainfall			resources	
Environment					

BRINGING THE RAIN TO KAPITI PLAIN

THE STORY

Ki Pat, a young cow-herd on the Kenyan plains ends the drought in his area. He fires an arrow with an eagle's feather into the cloud to make it drop its water. This story is told in rhyme.

QUESTIONS AND DISCUSSION

- What do the children think the person on the cover illustration is thinking?

- Ask pupils to describe the area.
  Is it good grass for cows to eat?
  What sort of climate does it appear to have?

MAPPING

- Show the children a map of Kenya.

  Ask them how many cities they can find and what size they are (population; square miles).

  Find the plains area and discuss how you might travel to the plains from the capital city, Nairobi.

EMPLOYMENT

- Draw an outline of Ki Pat and around it list all the jobs he must do as a cow herd.

- Interview or research the job of a British farmer.

- Compare Ki Pat's work with his British equivalent.

- Draw an outline of her/him as before, listing all the jobs carried out.
  What aspects of the jobs are similar and what aspects are different?

- Discuss what dangers there might be to Ki Pat's herd. (Disease, lack of water,

Jasmin

attack by wild animals, rustling).

What do the children think Ki Pat's people do about these dangers?

DROUGHT

- What could have been done to help the animals through the difficult time?

- What reasons can the children come up with to explain why they did not do any of the suggested things (e.g. not enough money, the local people did not expect the drought to be so bad).

In the past, the herds would have been moved around areas where the grazing is good even in times of drought.

CONSERVATION

Much of this land has now been taken up by this government for wildlife conservation areas or agriculture and the herds are denied access.

- Ask the pupils who benefits and who loses out from these changes.

  Consider :

  - wildlife for tourists,
  - farms for wealthy farmers,
  - income for the government,
  - income for local people.

- Role play or draw with speech bubbles to show the points of view of each of these groups.

NATIONAL CURRICULUM VOCABULARY TABLE

KEY STAGE 2

PHYSICAL GEOGRAPHY	WEATHER & CLIMATE	SETTLEMENTS	TRANSPORT	ECONOMIC ACTIVITIES	LOCATIONAL WORDS
Plain Grass Tree	Rain Drought Cloud Weather Thunder	City Town House Village		Job	Country Area Position Near/Far

KEY STAGE 2

PHYSICAL GEOGRAPHY	WEATHER & CLIMATE	SETTLEMENTS	TRANSPORT	ECONOMIC ACTIVITIES	LOCATIONAL WORDS
Landscape Vegetation Environment	Climate	Rural		Natural resources Tourism	Distribution

THE DAY OF AHMED'S SECRET

THE STORY

Ahmed is a young boy who works in Cairo delivering bottles of gas. He is thinking about his secret all day, while he works in the city. When he comes home to his family at night, he tells them his secret - he can write his name.

BUILDINGS AND STREETS

- Look at the illustrations in the book. What architectural features can you see?
    - ▪ Arches?   ▪ Balconies?
    - ▪ Stone walls?   ▪ Brick walls?
    - ▪ Domes?   ▪ Minarets?
    - ▪ Glass windows?

    Are these features similar to any in your own area?
    Are the same or different building materials used?

- What do any of these features tell you about the cultures, history and geography of the area?

- What examples of street furniture can you find in the book?
    - ▪ Lamp-posts?   ▪ Road signs?

    Are the streets narrow or wide?
    What are the advantages and disadvantages of narrow streets in a hot country, in a busy city, etc?

SETTLEMENT

- Does the part of Cairo that Ahmed travels through look crowded or quite empty?
    What about the part of the city around the pyramids?
    Do you think that all Cairo is like these pictures?
    Do you think that the pyramids would really have no-one around them?
    Which parts of your area are most like the busy parts of Cairo? What would you like about living somewhere as busy as that?

LANDSCAPE

- Different aspects of Cairo are shown in the pictures.
    Use a full map of Cairo to find the range of landscapes both urban and rural that you can find around Cairo.
    Inner city, suburbs, river-side, desert, farmland etc.
    Can you find the same range of landscapes in your area?

ENVIRONMENT

- Close your eyes as some of the story is read. Imagine what it would be like to be with Ahmed during the day.
    Describe the city in your own words, sounds, sights, smells etc.

- What do you see as the main environmental issue for people living in inner-city Cairo?
    Look at the Oxfam video *"Four Children and their City"*. How close were your guesses to what the children in the video said?

- Are the environmental issues in your area the same or different to those you see in Cairo?

EMPLOYMENT

- List all the things children do in a typical day.

  Chart under headings:
  - ✔ education
  - ✔ work
  - ✔ leisure
  - ✔ travel

  Give approximate time allocations for each.

- Do the same for Ahmed and discuss differences.

- Have a class discussion/role play on children working.

  What are the pros/cons?

  Do the class think it's right for children to work?

  If so, what kind of work, for how long, and at what age?

- Have a class debate.

  Let the children decide if they think children should be allowed to work or not.

  Ask children to sit on the left side of the room or the right depending on their point of view. One by one, ask the children stand up and argue their point of view.

  The children can get up and cross sides if their minds change during the debate.

- How many types of jobs can you see people doing in Cairo?

  What other jobs must people be doing in this area?

  What clues are there (eg. buildings)?

Candy

NATIONAL CURRICULUM VOCABULARY TABLE

KEY STAGE 1

PHYSICAL GEOGRAPHY	WEATHER & CLIMATE	SETTLEMENTS	TRANSPORT	ECONOMIC ACTIVITIES	LOCATIONAL WORDS
Sea	Wind	City	Cart	Work	Map
Sand		Building	Truck	Jobs	Country
Desert		House	Car	Shops	
River		Town	Caravans		
		Village	Bus		
			Boats		
			Moped		
			Walk		

KEY STAGE 2

PHYSICAL GEOGRAPHY	WEATHER & CLIMATE	SETTLEMENTS	TRANSPORT	ECONOMIC ACTIVITIES	LOCATIONAL WORDS
Relief	Temperature	Population		Markets	Globe
Landscape	Climate	Urban		Tourism	
Vegetation		Density			
Features					
Environment					

KATIE MORAG DELIVERS THE MAIL

THE STORY

Katie delivers the mail (five parcels) on a small Scottish island called Struay. She gets them mixed up and has to sort out the muddle.

TOURISM

- Do all the characters originally come from the island?

  Why did they move there?

  Where are the tourists from?

  What do the local people think of the tourists?

- Design a tourist brochure for an imaginary island or for Struay.

ISLANDS

- Look at pictures, maps, aerial photographs and books about islands.

- Make an island in the sand tray.

- Draw an imaginary island, putting in services i.e. post office, library.

- Discuss what effects living on a small island might have on people.

MAPPING

- Find Scotland on a map of the British Isles, a map of Europe, a world map and on a globe.

- Make parcels addressed to people in the school. Work out a route, then deliver them.

- Draw a map to show where Katie Morag went. Place a grid over the map and carry out work on co-ordinates.

QUALITY OF ENVIRONMENT

- List what the children think they would like or would not like if they lived in Struay.

- Compare with a list based on the children's likes and dislikes of the local area.

JOBS

- Invite the local postman/postwoman to come and talk to the class.

- Visit the local post office.

  Do a survey to find out why people have gone there.

STAMPS

- Start a class stamp collection.

  Compare stamps from different countries and classify under headings of those that show physical, human and environmental geography.

- Take a class vote for the most popular stamp.
- Design a school stamp or one for Struay showing the best features of the local area.

Sadek

NATIONAL CURRICULUM VOCABULARY TABLE

KEY STAGE 1

PHYSICAL GEOGRAPHY	WEATHER & CLIMATE	SETTLEMENTS	TRANSPORT	ECONOMIC ACTIVITIES	LOCATIONAL WORDS
Island		House	Boat	Post office	Map
Bay		Shop	Bridge	Farm	Aerial
Pool			Tractor	Service	photograph
			Journey		Country

KEY STAGE 2

PHYSICAL GEOGRAPHY	WEATHER & CLIMATE	SETTLEMENTS	TRANSPORT	ECONOMIC ACTIVITIES	LOCATIONAL WORDS
Environment			Route	Tourism	Globe
Features					Grid
					references
					Co-ordinates

MASAI AND I

LANGUAGE AND NAMES

● What do the Masai names Eshe, Hawa and Neema mean? Ask the children if their name has a meaning.

Do the children know anyone who has a name with meanings in other languages . *(use celebrities' names if children do not want to be put on the spot)*

● What does 'kraal' mean? What word in English is taken from this?

● What other words in English are taken from, or are the same as in other languages?

MAPPING

● Find East Africa on a globe.

Is it a country?

Find where the Masai live.

● On a world map, plot your journey to visit the Masai girl.
Contact airlines for routings.
Plan the most direct route.
How long would it take?

SETTLEMENT

● Does Linda live in a city?

List the evidence that indicates that she does.

● Do all East Africans live as the Masai girl does?
To answer this question, write to embassies (Tanzania, Kenya) for information and use books to research.

Sarah

● On a map show the area where the Masai live and where other East Africans live. What pattern emerges?

● What kind of settlement does the Masai girl live in?

CULTURAL DIFFERENCES

● Make a list to show the differences between the two cultures on

✔ housing

✔ travel

✔ food

✔ getting water

✔ telling the time.

● Make another list of the same topics to show the similarities.

KINSHIP

- What is kinship? Discuss Linda's feeling of kinship with the Masai. Why does she feel this way ?
- Ask the children to make a list of those they consider to be in their, or if they prefer, Linda's kin group.
- Have any of the children felt kinship with another person not related to them?

NATIONAL CURRICULUM VOCABULARY TABLE

KEY STAGE 1

PHYSICAL GEOGRAPHY	WEATHER & CLIMATE	SETTLEMENTS	TRANSPORT	ECONOMIC ACTIVITIES	LOCATIONAL WORDS
Cave	Rain	School	Street		Map
Sky		Flats	Car		
Soil		Kraal	Pedestrian		
Pasture		City	Journey		
Grassland		Settlement			
		House			

KEY STAGE 2

PHYSICAL GEOGRAPHY	WEATHER & CLIMATE	SETTLEMENTS	TRANSPORT	ECONOMIC ACTIVITIES	LOCATIONAL WORDS
Environment			Route		Globe
Climate					
Vegetation					
Landscape					

THE PEOPLE WHO HUGGED THE TREES

THE STORY

Amrita, an Indian girl, tried to protect her special tree against the axe. She was pushed out of the way and the tree was felled. Other people heard of what she had done and they all joined her, each hugging a tree in the woods to protect them. This classic folk tale is the basis for the ongoing Chipko Movement that set out to protect the forests.

QUESTIONS AND DISCUSSION

- Do any of the children have a special tree?

- Why is it special to them?

USING MAPS

- Find India on a map of the world. Find Rajastan on a map of India. Do any of your maps tell what that area is like?

- Make a 2D or 3D map of the place where the story is set.

- Using atlases and globes, locate other deserts in the world.

DESERT LIFE

- Find out more about deserts; where, how they were formed etc..

- Find out more about the problems of living in a desert environment.

- Discuss and investigate settlement patterns in desert areas.

TREES & WOOD

- Draw, or stick a picture of a tree on a large sheet of paper. Ask the children to write down around the tree all the things which trees give us and how they can help us (shelter from rain or sun, wood to build things from, etc.).

- Do a survey of the classroom and school and find all the things that are made or partly made from wood (hall floor, rulers, pencils, desks, etc.).

ROLE PLAY

- Read the story up to the part where the axeman is about to chop Amrita's tree. Stop reading and ask the children in groups to think of as many different ways that Amrita might use to try to stop the tree being chopped down.

- Photocopy some of the illustrations and ask the children to make speech or thought bubbles showing what they think the axemen and the villagers might be saying.

- Ask pupils to think of some other possible endings.

  What if, the Maharajah had killed Amrita? ...He chopped all the trees down?

- Tell the children that the prince is going to come and see the villagers, and they must tell him why he should not chop down the trees. The teacher leaves the room, saying the prince will be coming soon.

  The teacher returns in the role of the Maharajah and demands to know why they have stopped his men chopping down the trees.

- Ask the children to think of six questions they would like to ask Amrita, if they could meet her.

LOCAL ENVIRONMENT

- Ask the pupils if trees in their neighbourhoods are important.

  Do they have trees?

- What would they do if they saw someone breaking or chopping down a tree near their house or school?

- Find examples in the newspapers of people organising themselves to protect the environment in your locality.

  Compare the issues in the newspaper to those in the story.

- Find out about environmental protection groups that are like the Chipko Movement (for example Greenpeace, Friends of the Earth, or road protestors).

  Invite them for a visit to the school.

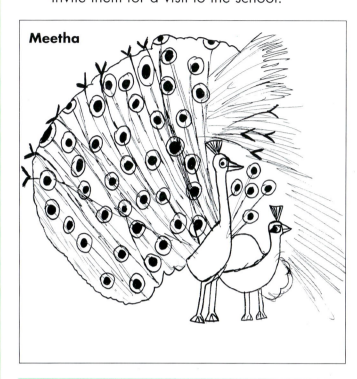

Meetha

And of course...
PLANT YOUR OWN SCHOOL TREE!

NATIONAL CURRICULUM VOCABULARY TABLE

KEY STAGE 1					
PHYSICAL GEOGRAPHY Land Soil Wood Forest	**WEATHER & CLIMATE** Season Desert Rain Weather Storm	**SETTLEMENTS** Settlement Village Building	**TRANSPORT**	**ECONOMIC ACTIVITIES** Work	**LOCATIONAL WORDS** Place Position

KEY STAGE 1					
PHYSICAL GEOGRAPHY Erosion Weathering Environment Vegetation Landscape	**WEATHER & CLIMATE** Climate Rainfall	**SETTLEMENTS**	**TRANSPORT**	**ECONOMIC ACTIVITIES** Labour Natural resources	**LOCATIONAL WORDS** Globe Region

SHAKER LANE

MAPPING

- Where is Shaker Lane?
  Think of possible countries and label these countries on a world map.
  Give reasons for choice.

- Devise a 2D or 3D Shaker Lane map taking clues from the book.
  Map the settlement at the beginning, middle and the end of the story.
  Discuss differences between pictures and maps.

LOCAL AREA

- Look at maps of your local environment from the present and from the past (even if only ten years before).
  List ways the map shows change.

- Visit a local building site.
  What used to be on the site?

- Interview someone (parent or neighbour) who knew the place before it changed.
  Why did it change?
  Divide the class into groups, giving each group a different brief such as housing, leisure, industry etc.
  What would they build on that site?
  Give reasons for their choice.
  Make a plan or model of each proposal.

- Using Shaker Lane as a 'known area', discuss similarities between it and the local environment.

ENVIRONMENTAL CHANGE

- Make a wall frieze depicting the changes that have taken place in Shaker Lane.

- Set up a role play between the country land agent and the residents. If possible, link in a local environmental issue e.g. a major road being built.

- Discuss the buildings of dams and the effects on people.
  Discuss how dams have changed the environment.
  Look at pictures of dams before and after construction.
  Make a dam using water in the sand tray.

RECYCLING

- Collect litter in the local environment around the school.

- Make up a (clean) rubbish bag and let the children sort items for recycling.

- Contact a local recycling group and invite a speaker.

- Set up a school can and paper bank.

- Make junk models/pictures/posters promoting recycling.

SETTLEMENT

- Why do people move?
  Have any of the children moved house?
  Why?
  How did they feel about moving?
  How did they move?
  What happened to the place they left?
- Describe the houses, land and buildings in the area of Shaker Lane.
  Which 'Shaker Lane' would the children prefer to live in .

- Why did people move to Shaker Lane?
  What were the houses like?

- What affects people's choice of location?

- Choose a character and in their words, explain why they moved to the area.

NATIONAL CURRICULUM VOCABULARY TABLE

KEY STAGE 1

PHYSICAL GEOGRAPHY	WEATHER & CLIMATE	SETTLEMENTS	TRANSPORT	ECONOMIC ACTIVITIES	LOCATIONAL WORDS
Stones		House	Road	Farm	Map
Field		Garden	Bridge	Dam	Country
Tree		Road	Crossroads	Reservoir	Plan
Hill		Building		Recycling	
		Settlement			

KEY STAGE 2

PHYSICAL GEOGRAPHY	WEATHER & CLIMATE	SETTLEMENTS	TRANSPORT	ECONOMIC ACTIVITIES	LOCATIONAL WORDS
Environment		Population		Fuel/power	Region
Floods				Energy	
				Natural resources	

SOMEWHERE IN AFRICA

THE STORY

Ashraf is a young boy who lives in a city in South Africa. He imagines lions and zebras in Africa's plains while wandering through his city on his way to the library where he renews his favourite book.

PRECONCEPTIONS

● Before reading the story, question the children, listing their ideas about what Africa is like.

● After reading the story, discuss how accurate their preconceptions were.

● Invite them to add to, or alter, their original list.

● Do people from outside the UK have different preconceptions of what it is like to live here? Look at books, UK tourist brochures, souvenirs etc.

Discuss the views of the UK they present compared with the children's own experiences.

MAPPING

● The story says Ashraf lives in a *'city, at the very tip of the great African continent.'*

Using an atlas or map of Africa, try and guess which city it is that Ashraf lives in.

● Make a jigsaw of Africa.
Photocopy an outline map.
The children then label the separate countries, colour, mount and cut out countries along borders to make jigsaw pieces.

● Make a 2D or 3D map of Ashraf's journey from his home to the library.
Place a grid over the 2D map for co-ordinate work.

WEATHER

● Survey weather in Britain and Southern Africa.

✔ Over a period of time record data from newspapers of temperature of capital cities of Southern African countries.

✔ Compare these with cities in UK.

✔ Produce a graph showing the collected data.

✔ Write statements about the findings relating to the climate and weather.

LOCAL AREA

● Ask the children to make a list of all the things they like about where they live.

● Draw an object from, or some part of, Ashraf's city. Put a tick on the items if they are in your local area too.

● List the jobs found in Ashraf's city. Compare with jobs found in the children's own locality.

● List the means of transport and buildings shown in Ashraf's city. Compare with the children's own environment.

UK STUDY

- Compare differences between the city and country in Ashraf's story.

- Do the same for the UK.
  What features are similar or different in both cities and countryside?

- Make a wall display using photos, travel posters, brochures and children's drawings showing these comparisons.

CONSERVATION

- Draw attention to the shop with tusks, tortoises etc.
  Ask why do/did people "need" these kinds of things?

Invite a speaker or send for information from

- ✔ The World Wildlife Fund

- ✔ Greenpeace

- ✔ Zoo Check

- ✔ Captive Animals Protection Society.

David

NATIONAL CURRICULUM VOCABULARY TABLE

KEY STAGE 1

PHYSICAL GEOGRAPHY	WEATHER & CLIMATE	SETTLEMENTS	TRANSPORT	ECONOMIC ACTIVITIES	LOCATIONAL WORDS
Grass	Summer	City	Street	Market	Continent
River	Sun	Shop	Traffic light	Supermarket	Map
Mud	Weather	Building	Car	Jobs	Plan
Plains			Alley		Country
Sky			Pedestrian		South

KEY STAGE 2

PHYSICAL GEOGRAPHY	WEATHER & CLIMATE	SETTLEMENTS	TRANSPORT	ECONOMIC ACTIVITIES	LOCATIONAL WORDS
Environment	Temperature	Urban		Conservation	Atlas
Vegetation	Climate	Port		Natural	
Landscape				resources	

WHERE THE RIVER BEGINS

THE STORY

Two boys and their grandad follow a river to its source. The story features a variety of scenery, weather and the different stages of the river's path.

QUESTIONS AND DISCUSSION

- Where could this story be set?

- Are there similar places in all areas of the world?

- How do you know?

- Why did the author chose only male characters for this story?

- How do the children feel about this?

MAPPING

- Name major rivers in England, Northern Ireland, Scotland and Wales and show on a map.

- Find major rivers on a variety of maps and globes (e.g. Amazon, Nile, Thames, Mississippi, Danube,)

- Make a plan or model of a river route showing changes from its source to the sea.

- Use compass points to plot a river route.

- Explore gradients of river taken from map evidence.

LOCAL AREA

- Visit a local river and make observations. Consider :
  - ✔ **the water**
  - ✔ **banks**
  - ✔ **soil**
  - ✔ **animal life**
  - ✔ **human use.**

  Visit the same river further up or down stream and compare observations.

- Identify some good and bad points of the local river and suggest improvements.

- Research the different forms of the transport of people and goods along the local river.

- Interview someone who uses or works on the local river
  (e.g. docker, river police, swimmer, ferry captain)

- Compare the local river study to the evidence shown in the illustrations in the book.

DEVELOPMENT

- What evidence of development can be seen in the book's illustrations (houses, agriculture, forest clearance)?

  How might this river change?

Akkas

Discuss and consider

- ✔ dams for power
- ✔ reservoirs
- ✔ riverside housing
- ✔ tourism
- ✔ bridges
- ✔ logging
- ✔ farming.

Make arguments for and against such changes.

WATER

- ● Find out how many forms of water exist in addition to rivers.
- ● Take water samples from
  - ✔ a river
  - ✔ the tap
  - ✔ rainwater
  - ✔ a spring
  - ✔ the sea
  - ✔ a pond
  - ✔ drain.

Compare water qualities.

NATIONAL CURRICULUM VOCABULARY TABLE

KEY STAGE 1

PHYSICAL GEOGRAPHY	WEATHER & CLIMATE	SETTLEMENTS	TRANSPORT	ECONOMIC ACTIVITIES	LOCATIONAL WORDS
Hill, River Forest, Field, Foothills Mountains Rocks, Pond Boulders Meadow Sea, Swell	Summer Sun, Hot Cold, Clouds Lightning, Thunder, Storm, Rain Flood	House Town Village	Transport Boats Bridge	Tourism Service Farm Logging Reservoir Jobs	Map Plan Up/Down

KEY STAGE 2

PHYSICAL GEOGRAPHY	WEATHER & CLIMATE	SETTLEMENTS	TRANSPORT	ECONOMIC ACTIVITIES	LOCATIONAL WORDS
Knoll Meander Upland Source Tributary River mouth Gradients	Dawn Mist		Route	Import Export Market	Globe Compass points Plot

BIBLIOGRAPHY

Gray, N, 1994,
A Balloon For Grandad
Orchard Books, ISBN 185213125X

Blathwayt, B, 1989,
Bear's Adventure
Julia MacRae, ISBN 0862033306

Verma, A, 1986,
Bringing The Rain To Kapiti Plain
Picture Mac, ISBN 0333351649

Heide, F.P and J, H. Gilliland 1991,
The Day Of Ahmed's Secret
Victor Gollancz, ISBN 0575050799

Hedderwick, M, 1989,
Katie Morag Delivers The Mail
The Bodley Head, ISBN 0370305698

Kroll, V, 1993,
Masai And I
Hamish Hamilton, ISBN 0241133114

Rose, D.L, 1990,
The People Who Hugged The Trees
Roberts Rinehart Publishers, ISBN 091197807

Provensen, A and M, 1987,
Shaker Lane
Julia MacRae, ISBN 0862033454

Mennen, I. and Daly, N.,1990
Somewhere in Africa
Bodley Head, ISBN 074452234X

Locker, T, 1984,
Where The River Begins
Patrick Hardy Books, ISBN 0744400473

FURTHER READING

Benedek, A. and Grunsell, A. (1994)
Cairo: Four Children And Their City
Oxfam (UK and Ireland)

Brennan, F. et. al.
Guidelines for good practice in development education
Development Education Support Centre, Dublin 1994.

Department of Education and Science (1986),
Geography from 5 to 16
HMI Series: Curriculum Matters 7. HMSO.

Long ago and far away: activities for using stories for history and geography at Key Stage 1
Development Education Centre (Birmingham), 1994.
ISBN 0 948838 28 0.

Start with a story : supporting young children's exploration of issues.
Development Education Centre (Birmingham), 1991.
ISBN 0 948838 20 5

Lewis, Elizabeth. I
Inside story: geography in children's books
"Primary Geographer" (series commencing 1994)

Midwinter, Cathy (Ed.).
Global perspectives in the National Curriculum: guidance for Key Stages 1 and 2
Development Education Association, 1995.
ISBN 1 900109 00 X

Nicholson, Heather Norris.
Place in story-time: geography through stories at Key Stages 1 and 2
The Geographical Association, 1994.
ISBN 0 948512 90 3

Redfern, Angela.
Starting with a story
Teacher Timesavers Series. Scholastic Publications Ltd., 1994.
ISBN 0-590-53129-8

UNICEF
Education for Development : a teacher's resource for global learning
Hodder & Stoughton, 1995

de Villiers, Mike (Ed.)
Primary geography matters: children's worlds
Keynote lectures and workshops from the GA's 1993 Centenary Annual Conference.
The Geographical Association,1993
ISBN 0 948512 62 8

Wallen, Margaret (Ed).
Every picture tells... : picture books as a resource for learning in all age groups
The National Association for the Teaching of English (NATE), 1990. ISBN 0 901291 18 8

USEFUL ADDRESSES

Development Education Association
29-31 Cowper Street, London EC2A 4AP
TEL: 0171 490 8108
FAX: 0171 490 8121

Can put you in touch with your local Development Education Centre

Development Education Dispatch Unit (DEDU)
153 Cardigan Road, Leeds LS6 1LJ
TEL: 0113 2784030
FAX: 0113 2744759
eMail: Resources @ Leedsdec.demon.co.uk

DEDU runs a mail order service of resources published by development education centres.

The Geographical Association
343 Fulwood Road, Sheffield S10 3BP
TEL: 0114 267 0666
FAX: 0114 267 0688

Greenpeace
Canonbury Villas, London N1 2PN
TEL: 0171 354 5100

Friends of the Earth
26-28 Underwood Street, London N1 7JQ
TEL: 0171 490 1555
FAX: 0171 490 0881